C000185250

Aphorisms

and

Thoughts

Napoleon Bonaparte

Selected by Honoré de Balzac

Translated by Charles D. Zorn

ONEWORLD
CLASSICS

ONEWORLD CLASSICS LTD
London House
243-253 Lower Mortlake Road
Richmond
Surrey TW9 2LL
United Kingdom
www.oneworldclassics.com

Maximes et pensées de Napoléon first published in 1838
First published by Oneworld Classics Limited in 2008
Translation © Charles D. Zorn, 2008

Printed in Great Britain by TJ International Ltd, Padstow,
Cornwall

ISBN: 978-1-84749-032-2

Contents

Preface by Honoré de Balzac   v

Aphorisms and Thoughts   1

Notes   102

Biographical Note   103

Note on the Text   109

Preface by Honoré de Balzac

T HE AUTHOR OF THIS WORK must confess
that his sole merit consists in the patience
with which he has, over several years, scoured
through books published on Napoleon and the
Moniteur archives, all the way down to the last
writings in which the words of this great sovereign have been recorded. Another merit is to
have perceived the importance of the work re-
sulting from it, which is to Napoleon what the
Gospel is to Jesus Christ. Indeed, this book,
which will be a treasure trove for many people,
would have lost some of its value if all of Napoleon's thoughts had been published indis-
criminately. La Rochefoucauld certainly did
not make available the entirety of the maxims
suggested to him by events: he selected, studied,
weighed up and compared those that he handed
down to us; whereas Napoleon did not think of

formulating a body of doctrine. The sub-lieutenant spoke without knowing the prime consul, the Emperor often had thoughts without foreseeing St Helena. It was also not an ordinary task to extract the man from each circumstance and to know his real thoughts through the conflicts into which the circumstances of his life had dragged him.

There was nothing to hesitate about in this choice: Napoleon is one of the most violent wills known in the annals of human domination: therefore there could be nothing more interesting about him than the rules by which he constructed and maintained his power.

However, from his starting point to his final destination, and from his throne to his tomb, he twice travelled, and in two different directions, the entire social state, which he managed to see and observe in its entirety; every time one of his words, as removed as it might be from politics, appeared to us fundamentally to light up certain episodes of human life, we have not omitted it: thus anyone will find here something useful to them, big or small, as this mind, as sharp as a sword, has sounded every depth. The terrorist of '93 and the general-in-chief have been absorbed by the Emperor, the governor has often refuted the governed; but the phrases which the various crises tore from him and which collide against each other admirably reveal the great struggle to which he was condemned. Also, a single phrase in this collection often portrays certain phases of his life and several portions of contemporary history much better than historians have achieved until now. Can the book of the man who deliberates after the fact ever be worth the cry of the man struck in his heart? What poetry the pain of Napoleon!

Still it was necessary to prune several thoughts which were shared by the great people who preceded him in politics, and others from which his name did not take away their commonness. Nevertheless, we have provided the ones the Emperor has repeated often enough to impress on them the seal of fact; do they not consequently explain his genius, his opinions or his domination?

In the eyes of the masses, this book will be like an apparition: the soul of the Emperor will pass in front of them; but, for certain chosen minds, it will be his history in algebraic form: the abstract man will be visible in it, the Idea in lieu of the Action. Will it not be one of the most singular events in the destiny of this man that, after having so vigorously struggled against the manifestation of thought, he himself ends up being a mere book? This collection of axioms will above all be the guidebook of endangered powers: no one has had a better instinct for peril in the act of governing than Napoleon. We will do him the justice of recognizing that he was frank, and never shrank back from any consequence: he glorified Action and condemned Thought. That is in two words the spirit of this political testament. Many of these maxims will also seem Machiavellian, cruel, false, and will be criticized by many of those who in themselves take them to be just and ready to be applied. It is not unnecessary to point out that Napoleon never contradicted himself in his hatred for lawyers, idealists and republicans. His opinion with regard to them amounts to banishing public discussion from government affairs.

We are not to take sides here for or against the experience that this great man has bequeathed to France: it is not up to anyone to defend or accuse Napoleon, it is enough to make him appear in front of all of us. His thoughts constitute a legislation which will be censured or adopted, but which had to be brought up to date in its most concise form; nobody will forget that they contain the secrets of the greatest organizer of modern times; if they are in direct opposition to France's current spirit, this vigorous contradiction was one further motive to publish them. Napoleon considered responsible governing to be impossible and press freedom as incompatible with the existence of power: what kind of flattery will be in store for the kings and ministers who will solve a problem they proclaimed was insoluble?

There is one more thing left to say about the divisions that we have made in this mass of thoughts, the suitability of which will, we hope, be well received.

It seemed to us possible to determine which maxims and ideas Napoleon came up with before 18th Brumaire, that is to say, while he was still a republican or citizen, subject or subservient to a recognized power.

After this first portion, we have put together all the thought concerning the art of warfare, which was the secret to his rise and the engine of his empire's power.

The third part contains all the ideas about the sovereign and those which the exercise of his power or his organization must have suggested to him.

Finally, the fourth is everything which experience and adversity have prescribed to him, it is the cry of the modern Prometheus.

If Napoleon is remarkable politically, it is thanks to his predictions on the state of Europe. Today his greatest enemies or those who sought to belittle him could not disagree that the eagle-eyed vision with which he embraced the battlefield also reached the broadest fields of politics; today the majority of the predictions he pronounced on the future events of Europe and the world have been accomplished; as for the rest, there is no doubt for superior minds that they will be accomplished.

(This is an edited version of Balzac's original 1838 preface to the collection, published under the name "J.-L. G***y jeune".)

Aphorisms
and
Thoughts

1

There are only two classes in Europe: that which wants privileges and that which rejects them.

2

If obedience is the result of the instinct of the masses, then rebellion is the result of their reflection.

3

A revolution is an opinion which discovers bayonets.

4

A revolution is a vicious circle: it starts with excess only to return to it.

5

The young fulfil the revolutions which the old have prepared.

6

The greatest republican is Jesus Christ.

7

In times of revolution one forgets everything.

8

Pitt was the banker for the French civil war and Revolution.

9

Most countries' laws were made to oppress the unfortunate and to protect the powerful.

10

Robespierre has been, in many respects, an honest man.

11

It is rare that a great assembly is reasonable: it is too readily passionate.

12

A club cannot support one enduring leader: it needs one for every interest.

13

Collective crimes make no one answerable.

14

Every assembly tends to turn the sovereign into a ghost and the population into a slave.

15

All great assemblies can be reduced to several cliques, and each clique to one man.

16

People are capable of judgement when they do not listen to sermonizers; lawyers will never save anything and will always be on the losing side.

17

If Louis XVI had stood trial before a counter-revolutionary court, he would have been found guilty.

18

When Louis XVI was put on trial, he should simply have said that according to law his person was sacred, and left it at that. This would not have saved his life, but he would have died as King.

19

Charles I perished for having resisted, Louis XVI for not having resisted; neither of the two understood the power of inertia, which is the secret of all great reigns.

20

A prince accused by his subjects owes them no apologies.

21

Those who take revenge out of principle are fierce and unrelenting.

22

All parties are Jacobins.

23

The Red Caps went further than the monarchy in terms of absolute power.

24

Without justice there are only oppressors and victims, and during revolutions there can be no justice.

25

These days, you can debase yourself even while oppressing.

26

During the Revolution, the French were never without a king.

27

Robespierre was a case of trial and sentence without plea.

28

During the Revolution, everything was up for grabs between thirty million people.

29

The wars of the Revolution have ennobled the entire French nation.

30

In revolutions there are only two types of people: those who carry them out and those who profit from them.

31

The highest of all virtues is devotion to the fatherland.

32

The large landowning aristocracy was only good and possible in the feudal system.

33

Aristocracy is in the Old Testament; democracy in the New Testament.

34

The protocol of address between nations is different to that between individuals.

35

The majority of sentiments are traditions.

36

The hereditary nature of nobility takes away emulation from the noblemen and the bourgeois.

37

The man who has joined a party is the man with the least freedom.

38

The recourse to foreigners is a criminal act.

39

A party which sustains itself only through foreign bayonets will be defeated.

40

In France freedom is in the charter and slavery in the law.

41

There will never be any social revolution without terror.

42

The ambition to dominate minds is the strongest of all passions.

43

Every hour of time wasted during youth creates a chance for future misfortune.

44

A great reputation is a great noise; the more you make, the more it spreads: laws, nations, monuments – everything crumbles; but the noise remains.

45

He who practises virtue solely in the hope of achieving great renown decidedly borders on vice.

46

Man only succeeds in life by governing his character or by forging one.

47

The characteristic of any method should be assisting conception, facilitating memory and giving more power to thought.

48

Misfortune is the midwife of genius.

49

Strong spirits turn away from sensual pleasures just as seafarers avoid reefs.

50

The superior man is impassive: praise him or condemn him, he always carries on.

51

There is no strength without dexterity.

52

In France we admire only the impossible.

53

You are much more likely to amuse men with absurdities than with reasonable ideas.

54

You only believe that which it pleases you to believe.

55

In an settled sphere, great men are trouble-makers.

56

The way to be believed is to make truth un-believable.

57

A beautiful woman appeals to the eye, a good woman appeals to the heart; one is a jewel, the other a treasure.

58

The nobility would have survived if it had looked after its branches more than its roots.

59

The majority of those who do not want to be oppressed want to be oppressors themselves.

60

In science, the world of details is there to be discovered.

61

How many men are guilty only because of weakness for their women!

62

There should be neither passion nor prejudice in the pursuit of one's business; this can only be permitted for the sake of public good.

63

A man without courage or bravery is only a thing.

64

Exposure to the most violent events does not wear out the heart as much as abstractions do: soldiers are worth more than lawyers.

65

Out of a hundred of those favoured by kings, ninety-five have been hanged.

66

Love is foolishness committed by two people.

67

The nobility would have survived if it had known how to master the writing desk.

68

Bravery succeeds as often as it fails: thanks to it there are equal opportunities in life.

69

Europe is a molehill; there have only ever been great empires in the Orient, where there are six hundred million people.

70

Muhammad's superiority consisted in having founded a religion without a hell.

71

In Egypt, under a good administration, the Nile wears away at the desert; under a bad administration, the desert wears away at the Nile. The genie of evil and the genie of good are always present there: in this lies the whole of Egypt.

72

A desert is an ocean of dry land.

73

If I had conquered Acre I would have triggered a revolution in the Orient.

74

We can kill the Turks, but we will not defeat them.

75

There are only two countries: the East and the West; two peoples: the Easterners and the Westerners.

76

I am one of those who believes that the sorrows of the other world have only been imagined as a complement to the insufficient attractions that are presented to us there.

77

The men who have changed the universe never achieved this by addressing themselves to the leaders, but by stirring the masses. The former method is just intrigue, and only generates secondary results. The latter method is the way of a genius, and changes the face of the world.

78

There are only two levers to stir men: fear or self-interest. Every great revolution must act on fear; when the interests are at stake, great results do not follow. (*This thought is a demonstration, of sorts, of no. 41.*)

79

Democratic government borders on anarchy, monarchy on despotism; anarchy is powerless, despotism can accomplish great things.

80

Good republics cannot be made out of old monarchies.

81

There are so many laws that no one is exempt from being hanged.

82

Parties are weakened by their fear of competent people.

83

Aggressors may be wrong in the hereafter, but they are right on earth.

84

You can only do well what you do yourself.

85

In France, salvation for all resides in the eradication of political parties.

86

To confer in the midst of danger is like pulling on the reins.

87

The people must be saved against their will.

88

The superior man follows nobody else's path.

89

One exults in oneself when in danger.

90

Nothing has been founded merely by the sword.

91

You never climb that high unless you do not know where you are going.

92

To say where I come from, who I am, where I am going, is beyond me, and yet all this is fact.

93

You can only lead the people by showing them a future: a leader trades in hope.

94

Success is the world's greatest orator.

95

You can only vanquish need with absolute power.

96

I will be the Brutus of kings and the Caesar of the Republic.

97

He who saves his homeland breaks not a single law.

98

A revolution is accomplished when the only thing remaining to be done is to get rid of one man.

99

Nothing works in a political system in which words clash with things.

100

Success makes a man great.

101

War is a state of nature.

102

Coldness is the greatest quality of a man destined to command.

103

Bravery is an innate quality: it cannot be acquired, it stems from the blood. Courage comes from thought; bravery is often merely restlessness in the face of danger.

104

One is only brave for the sake of others.

105

Courage cannot be counterfeited: it is a virtue which escapes hypocrisy.

106

The burst of courage which, despite the suddenness of events, still leaves you capable of thought, of judgement and of decision, is excessively rare.

107

Where there is the flag, there is France.

108

The foremost quality of a soldier is his capacity for withstanding fatigue; courage only comes second to this.

109

The best soldier is not so much the one who fights but the one who marches.

110

Hardship and misery are the soldier's true teachers.

111

Of all people, the soldier is the most sensitive to acts of benevolence.

112

For the brave man a musket is merely a handle for his bayonet.

113

There are five things which should never leave a soldier's hands: his musket, his ammunition, his satchel, at least four days' worth of supplies and his pickaxe.

114

Why go for an epaulette on a battlefield when you can get one in an antechamber?

115

Discipline can only last if it is appropriate to the national character.

116

At war, genius is thought in action.

117

War is above all a matter of tact.

118

War is a lottery in which nations should stake only small amounts.

119

You become the man of your uniform.

120

There are no men who get on better together than soldiers and priests.

121

There is only one honourable way of being taken prisoner: when in isolation and unable to use your weapons. Then there is no compromise and you submit to necessity.

122

A general under the power of the enemy has no more orders to give to those who are still fighting.

123

It is against all policies to authorize officers and even generals to capitulate when they are taken by surprise or surrounded, except when a garrison is under siege; as a rule you should always fight on, even when all hope seems lost.

124

At war, any commander who surrenders one moment earlier than he is obliged to deserves death.

125

Nothing increases a battalion like success.

126

The military science consists in the calculation of masses on given points.

127

At war, audacity is genius's most splendid calculation.

128

At war you should press upon an obstacle in order to overcome it.

129

It is imagination which loses battles.

130

A general must be a charlatan.

131

There are men who, because of their physical and moral constitution, tend to schematize everything: whatever their knowledge, courage or intellect, Nature has not brought them here to command an army.

132

An esteemed general's gesture is worth more than the finest harangue.

133

An army is a population that obeys.

134

A conscripted army will end up capitulating.

135

An army must at all times be ready to counter the level of resistance of which it is itself capable.

136

In war, as in love, to get it over with you have to
get closer.

137

In war, theory is good for providing general ideas,
but the strict application of these guidelines will
always involve danger: they are the axes which
must serve to draw the curve.

138

There are only two kinds of war strategies: good
ones and bad ones; the good ones almost always
fail due to unforeseen circumstances, which
often make the bad ones succeed.

139

Woe betide the general who comes to the battlefield with a system.

140

He who does not view a battlefield without tears
lets many men die needlessly.

141

At the outset of a campaign you have to consider carefully whether you should move forwards or not, but once the offensive has been launched, it must be followed through to its furthest limit. However adeptly you manoeuvre in retreat, it will weaken the troops' morale, since by diminishing the chances of success you place them in the enemy's hands. Besides, retreats are even more costly in terms of human lives and equipment than the most bloody skirmishes; with the difference that, in a battle, the enemy's losses are approximately the same as yours, whereas in a retreat you lose without the other party losing.

142

A general-in-chief should say to himself several times a day: if the enemy army appeared in front of me, to my right, to my left, what would I do? And if he finds himself at a loss, he is on a bad track, he is out of order, he has to set it right.

143

In an army the infantry, the cavalry and the artillery must be in the right proportions: one weapon cannot compensate for another; there should always be one artillery piece for every thousand men, and the cavalry should amount to a quarter of the infantry.

144

Never start a sideways manoeuvre in front of an army in position. This principle is absolute.

145

The strength of an army, like the quantity of movement in mechanics, can be calculated by multiplying the mass by the speed. A rapid march increases the morale of the army; it raises its chances of success.

146

A cannon should have three hundred shots to fire, which is its consumption in two battles.

147

There are cases in which expending men's lives saves blood.

148

Infantry is the soul of the army.

149

The infantry must shoot at the cavalry from afar, instead of waiting for it at point-blank range.

150

In the current state of composition of the infantry, you should give more consistency to the third rank or remove it entirely.

151

The secret of great battles consists in knowing how to stretch out and regroup at will.

152

The principles of Caesar were those of Hannibal, and those of Hannibal were those of

Alexander: keeping your forces together, not being vulnerable at any point, rapidly bringing all your forces to bear on a given point.

153

The art of war, with a smaller army, consists in always having more forces than the enemy at the spot where you are attacking or being attacked.

154

Left to their own devices, the infantry and the cavalry will not come to any definite result; but with artillery, in equal numbers, the cavalry will destroy the infantry.

155

Artillery is everything in battle as in a siege; once the fray has begun, the skill consists in making a large amount of gunfire converge on the same point, without the enemy being able to predict it.

156

As a rule, an army must always keep its columns together so that the enemy cannot wedge itself between them; if for some important reason this rule is abandoned, the detached units must be independent in their operations and manoeuvre towards a fixed spot, on which they converge without hesitation and without needing new orders.

157

The art of positioning a camp is nothing more than the art of finding a battle line there; the position taken must neither be overlooked, nor stretched, nor enveloped, and on the contrary must overlook, stretch and envelop the opposing force.

158

One must never detach any corps from an army the day before an attack; everything can change from one moment to the other: one battalion can determine the outcome of an entire day.

159

During a campaign, no leader should sleep in a house, and there should be only one tent, that of the general-in-chief, because of his maps.

160

The greatest danger occurs in the moment of victory.

161

An enemy in flight must either be given easy passage or be met with a wall of steel. (*1813. Vandamme Affair*)

162

Politics and morality are in agreement when it comes to rejecting pillaging.

163

The only possible change for modern armies is the suppression of logistical problems – the magazines, the ovens, the wagons, the luggage – which so troubled the ancients.

164

The great revolution yet to be brought into the military art will come from the solution that needs to be found for giving the soldier as much flour as possible to carry and the equipment to make him cook it – which had always preoccupied Caesar.

165

Artillery is still too heavy, too complicated: there is still more to simplify and reduce.

166

Kindness and honest treatment honour the victor and dishonour the loser, who should stay on his own and owe nothing to pity. (*1798. Letter to Kléber*)

167

The loss of our naval battles is due to the generals-in-chief's lack of character, tactical weaknesses and the attitude of the captains, who believe they must only act upon signal.

168

The first law of naval tactics must be that as soon as the admiral has given the signal to attack, each captain must move to attack an enemy vessel and support his neighbouring ships.

169

If an army ever enters England, London will not be able to resist for even an hour.

170

Hannibal forced his way through the Alps the first time around; I bypassed them.

171

The Germans, and especially the Austrians, do not know the value of time.

172

You do not find intrepid people among those who have something to lose.

173

Danger gives spirit to the French.

174

François I had a fine and formidable artillery unit at Pavia; he placed his cavalry in front and blocked his batteries which, if they had fired, would have given him victory; he failed to uphold the principle that an army must at any moment provide the resistance of which it is capable.

175

My finest campaign was that of 20th March: not a single musket shot was fired.

176

Equality exists only in theory.

177

The name and the form of a government do not mean anything, just as long as the citizens have equal rights and justice is well served.

178

If one analyses it, political freedom is an accepted myth thought up by those governing to send the governed to sleep.

179

Social law can give all men equal rights; nature will never give them equal faculties.

180

Monarchy is founded on the inequality of conditions that are in nature, and the republic on an equality which is impossible.

181

The people will never choose true legislators.

182

Absolute power represses or promotes ambitions selectively, democracy unchains them all without discrimination.

183

Democracy elevates sovereignty, aristocracy only preserves it.

184

A usurper has had too many masters not to exert absolute power from the outset.

185

Nothing should resemble a man less than a king.

186

In the system of absolute power only one voice is necessary to rectify an injustice; in the assembly system five hundred are necessary.

187

The foundation of any authority lies in the advantages offered to those who obey.

188

Taking all things into consideration, you must be of a military disposition in order to govern; you can only govern a horse with boot and spur.

189

There is no such thing as absolute despotism; it can only be relative. Excess spills over on one side or the other: the territory the ocean gains is lost elsewhere.

190

Absolute power must be paternal in nature, otherwise it will be overthrown.

191

The best link between people and their prince is happiness.

192

Without a master, the mere words "people's rights" are a crime in politics.

193

Any man who is worth thirty million and is willing to dispense with it is dangerous for a government.

194

A sovereign must never make promises he intends to keep.

195

A government can only live on its principles.

196

It is unanimity of interest that makes a government strong.

197

Good politics is making the people believe that they are free; good government is making them happy according to their wishes.

198

The sovereign should only be seen in full action, granting favours and devoid of any infirmities.

199

In the eyes of the founders of empires, men are not men but instruments.

200

The torment of precaution is worse than the dangers it seeks to avoid: it is better to abandon yourself to destiny.

201

A prince who is afraid is liable to be overthrown at any moment.

202

A sovereign obliged to respect the law can witness the death of his state.

203

You can lose popularity with a peccadillo just as with a great coup d'état: when you know the art of ruling you only risk your credit in reputable establishments.

204

A newborn government must dazzle.

205

Populations need noisy celebrations: fools like noise, and the multitude are fools.

206

A head of state should in his conscience foresee events; the moment he is the most magnanimous, he is accused of tyranny.

207

To listen to everyone's interests is the sign of an ordinary government; to foresee them is that of a great government.

208

Everything must be unified in the restoration of a state. It is not enough to join up factions by transforming their passions into common interests; it is half the task at most if you don't also connect these interests to the other ones. In order to be master at home, you mustn't be afraid of condemning party divides.

209

A parliament is good for obtaining from the people what the king cannot ask from it.

210

A sovereign must take care to find good in evil, and vice-versa.

211

The head of a state cannot be the head of a party.

212

The rank of sovereigns depends on that of their peoples.

213

A great sovereign is one who foresees results at any given moment.

214

A sovereign who ties himself to a faction tips the barge and hastens the shipwreck.

215

Old and corrupt nations are not governed like the ancients; for every person willing to sacrifice himself for the good of the public, there are today thousands who only know their own interests and vanity. The legislator's and the sovereign's secret is to make good use of the vices they must reign over – there lies one of the secrets of the return to crosses and cords. We have come to the point where distinctions command respect for oneself while satisfying one's own vanity.

216

Honour is a moral treasury for the sovereign.

217

The more the sovereign is absolute, the more dangerous palace militias are.

218

A circumstantial law is an accusation against the ruling power.

219

Government must continually prove itself.

220

Transactions demean power.

221

Any government must solely view men en masse.

222

It is of great necessity for a government to be harsh after a great revolution.

223

In all public actions one needs strength, consistency and unity.

224

The head of state must make even evil contribute to the triumph of public affairs.

225

With happiness you make a people glorious; much consistency is needed to make it happy.

226

One must display more character while administering than at war.

227

Etiquette is the king's prison.

228

A government formed of disparate elements will not last.

229

There are people who only behave themselves in front of their enemy.

230

I do not like those who claim to scorn death; what is essential is to know how to suffer what is inevitable.

231

In the application of laws, you must know how to calculate the unproductive elements.

232

It is possible to be enough of a non-believer not to believe in the benefits of communion, and still be just enough of a believer not to expose yourself blatantly to sacrilege. (*Upon coronation*)

233

The irritability of a government reveals its weakness.

234

A throne is nothing but a plank covered in velvet.

235

There is a kind of netting over the lower classes which envelops the multitudes; a link has to break for something to rise from it.

236

The interests of the state sooner or later prevail over small passions.

237

In government affairs, a false bud often leads, with the help of some adjustment, to a true result.

238

Ordinarily a benefactor demands more than he gives.

239

A sovereign must trust neither words nor faces.

240

Statistics is the balancing-out of things.

241

The separation of the treasury and the finance ministry is the true specialization, the only possible one.

242

For a people to be free, those governed would have to be wise and those governing be gods.

243

Conspirators who come together to overthrow a tyranny start by submitting to that of their leader.

244

The clergy would be the best educational body if they could only renounce their foreign leader.

245

You can only escape the arbitrariness of a judge by placing yourself under the despotism of law.

246

Morality is in itself an entire code of law.

247

It is by hurting the self-esteem of princes that you can influence their deliberations.

248

No man can tell what he will do in his final moments.

249

The head of a state can no more abandon the government of ideas than that of men.

250

Since the discovery of printing, the enlightened have been consulted in order to rule, while one only rules in order to subjugate them.

251

If science was led by the hand of power, it would provide great results for society.

252

There are inevitable revolutions. They are moral eruptions, like the physical eruptions of volcanoes. When the chemical combinations that produce the latter are complete, they explode, just as revolutions do when the moral combinations are in place; to prevent them, the movement of ideas must be monitored.

253

There are no ideals that do not leave a positive residue.

254

A sovereign must always appropriate publicity for his own benefit.

255

The Idea has caused more harm than the Action: it is the prime enemy of sovereigns.

256

A physical conspiracy is put to an end once the hand that holds the dagger is seized; a moral conspiracy has no end.

257

Classic works are composed by rhetoricians, whereas they should be composed only by men of state or men of the world.

258

A people that can say anything can manage to do anything.

259

Newspapers should be reduced to small notices.

260

Books lead to too much reasoning for them to avoid corrupting a nation by getting it out of the habit of action.

261

Great authors are esteemed prattlers.

262

A book in which there are no lies would be a curious one.

263

A fool is merely boring, a pedant is unbearable.

264

Everyone wants rulers to be just, and no one is just towards them.

265

You cannot do anything with a philosopher.

266

An atheist is a better subject than a fanatic: one obeys, the other kills.

267

Sovereigns must forgive mistakes and never forget them.

268

Men are better governed by their vices than by their virtues.

269

Men are grateful for being surprised, whereas happiness seems to be owed to them.

270

Honest men are so peaceful, rogues are so alert, that they must often be well employed.

271

Show a rogue in public and he will act like an honest man.

272

There are rogues who are roguish enough to conduct themselves as honest people.

273

In politics, young people are worth more than old people.

274

The best way to keep your word is never to give it.

275

The phrase "political virtue" is a nonsense.

276

A prince must suspect everything.

277

A state finds itself better off by persisting with mediocre ministers who stay in place than by often changing ministers, even if it chooses great minds.

278

Theological volcanoes are cooled with water, not oil.

279

It is not for circumstances to rule politics, but for politics to rule circumstances.

280

The indecision of princes is to governments what paralysis is to the movement of limbs.

281

One can risk a coup d'état in order to seize power, never to consolidate it; one would be striking at a sovereign.

282

In politics, absurdity is not an obstacle.

283

Neutrality consists in weighing everyone on the same scale; in politics it is a nonsense: one man's triumph is always in the best interest.

284

Those who cannot be rewarded must be disgraced.

285

To fear death is to profess one's atheism.

286

The Church must be within the State, and not the State within the Church.

287

The candles that are lit in full daylight today once lit up catacombs. (*In Notre-Dame, the day of his coronation*)

288

In politics, there are situations you can only get out of by wrongdoing.

289

Inevitable wars are always just.

290

It is easier to make laws than to apply them.

291

The police invents more than it finds.

292

It is easier to deceive than to undeceive.

293

The most dangerous form of power is an abstract entity behind the forces of law and order.

294

Marriage does not stem from nature.

295

With audacity you can attempt everything – you cannot do everything.

296

To interpret a law is to corrupt it; lawyers kill laws.

297

A bad law applied does a better service than a good law interpreted.

298

It is by knocking heads together that people get to know each other.

299

There is nothing more difficult to harness than a population that has shaken off its yoke.

300

A throne can neither be raised again nor consolidated with sabre strokes.

301

The only victory against love is flight.

302

How do we know that animals do not have their own language?

303

Plants are also animals that eat and drink.

304

Interest is only the key to base actions.

305

Interminable matters are those which present no difficulties.

306

Men who debase themselves do not conspire.

307

Some vices and virtues can depend on circumstance.

308

The sovereign is always wrong to speak in anger.

309

How can you not be good if you can do everything?

310

It is foolish to want to establish legal responsibility
for actions in politics.

311

A parish priest must be a natural judge of peace,
the moral leader of the population.

312

Moral cynicism is the ruin of the body politic.

313

It is a principle that authorities and garrisons
must be moved around; state interest requires
that there should be no immovable posts: unity
of thought must not exist in one place only.

314

There are some types of wrongs which tribunals cannot address, and modern laws have tied the hands of sovereigns on these matters.

315

You should neither constrain nor take action against shortcomings which are not harmful.

316

An empire like France can and must have some hospices for madmen, known as charterhouses.

317

The ancients cumulated professions and we separate them.

318

If perfection was not illusory, it would not have so much success.

319

He who can absorb the most images into his memory is the one who has the most imagination.

320

There are no possible laws against money.

321

You can thwart many things by pretending not to see them.

322

Politics, which cannot be moral, must make morality triumph.

323

Men model themselves according to circumstance.

324

There is nothing more imperious than weakness which feels itself supported by force.

325

Envy is a confession of inferiority.

326

Perversity is never shared.

327

Human weaknesses must be recognized and adapted to rather than fought.

328

Can we make God the object of our discussions here on earth?

329

Cunning does not always announce weakness.

330

These days, an appeal is nothing but a dispute between a ruling and the law.

331

Accomplished courtiers must scorn their idol and be ready to destroy him.

332
He who can flatter can also slander.

333
It is quite difficult to know where politeness ends and flattery begins.

334
Money is more powerful than despotism.

335
Circumstantial laws are abolished by new circumstances.

336
In world affairs it is not faith that will save us: it is mistrust.

337
Diplomacy amounts to police in grand costume.

338
Such and such a lady of the old aristocracy will give her body to a plebeian but will not reveal

the secrets of the aristocracy to him; in the same way people of a certain rank are the only possible ambassadors.

339

Treaties are executed as long as interests are at one with another.

340

To impose excessively harsh conditions on someone is to exempt them from fulfilling them.

341

A conference is a myth agreed on between diplomats: it is Machiavelli's quill combined with Muhammad's sabre.

342

Old people who preserve the tastes of their youth lose in consideration what they gain in ridicule.

343
Novels are the history of human desires.

344
Labour is Time's scythe.

345
There are no such things as minor events for nations and sovereigns.

346
Peoples in motion cannot be stopped.

347
Love is the idle man's occupation, the soldier's distraction and the sovereign's pitfall.

348
One should not buy a dubious ally at the expense of a faithful ally.

349
Fools speak of the past, wise men of the present and madmen of the future.

350

Any indulgence towards culprits implies connivance.

351

The system is to power what the service is to religion.

352

It is not easy to obtain simplicity with practitioners of law: the formalists in the State Council prevented many simplifications.

353

Man's disquiet is such that he absolutely needs the vagueness and mystery religion provides him.

354

A religious nation is crushed, not divided.

355

Charters are only good as long as they are made to work.

356

Madness is characterized by the discrepancy between visions and faculties.

357

A man with a smooth brow has never reflected.

358

Commerce unites men; everything that unites them makes them gang up: commerce is essentially harmful to authority.

359

Any society is a government within government.

360

Beggars are small-time monks.

361

Wealth does not consist in the possession but in the use of treasure.

362

Family organization does not stem from natural law: marriage takes its shape from custom.

363

With regard to marriage, the eastern family is entirely different from the western family: morality is therefore not universal. Man is the minister of nature and society grafts itself onto it.

364

Marriage is not always the result of love; the majority of young people get married in order to achieve independence, a household, and take on spouses who do not suit them at all. The law must provide them with a resource for when they realize that they have made an absolute mistake; but this facility must favour neither fickleness nor passion: a woman must only be able to divorce once and not get remarried before five years have elapsed. After ten years of marriage, divorce must be impossible.

365

In order to be happy, marriage requires a continuous exchange of sweat.

366

Gall* pre-existed in these proverbial phrases: linnet head, square head.

367

It is a great wrong at Court not to put yourself forward.

368

Laws that are clear in theory are often chaotic in their application.

369

From intelligence to good sense, it is often further than you think.

370

Severity prevents even more mistakes than it reprimands.

371

Every good law must be short; if long, it becomes a set of regulations.

372

What is called natural law is nothing but the law of interest and reason.

373

There are crises in which the good of the people requires the condemnation of an innocent.

374

Habit condemns us to a fair number of follies, and the greatest of these is to become enslaved to them.

375

You must follow Fortune in its whims and correct it when you can.

376

Anything which is not founded on physically and mathematically exact bases must be banished by reason.

377

Every work of intellect is all the more superior when the author is universal.

378

A good philosopher makes a bad citizen.

379

Conspiracies are made for the benefit of the most cowardly.

380

It is never useful to stoke up embers.

381

When ruling you must govern with the head, never with the heart.

382

Everything in life is subject to calculation.

383

The populace judges the power of God by the power of the priests.

384

Morality is quite often the passport for malicious gossip.

385

The fool has a great advantage over the man of intellect: he is always pleased with himself.

386

When you detect a moral ailment, you must learn to treat the soul as you would treat an arm or a leg.

387

In politics as in war, any wrong, even if within the rules, is only excusable as long as it is necessary.

388

Foreign trade, in its results infinitely below industry and agriculture, is designed for them, while both the latter are not designed for the former. The interests of these three essential bases for the prosperity of the state are different and often at odds: they must only be dealt with in their natural order.

389

A statesman's heart must be in his head.

390

The poor man and the beggar are two quite different classes: one commands respect, the other arouses anger.

391

When within a society everyone wants a post, you finds yourself having been sold in advance.

392

Education and history are enemies of religion.

393

A man fights more for his interests than for his rights.

394

Foreign matrimonial alliances never guarantee or ensure anything.

395

One way to suppress half of all court cases would be to pay only the lawyers who win their case – but I could never pass this idea by the State Council.

396

Love is the lot of idle societies.

397

In the realm of imagination as well as that of calculation, the power of the unknown is immeasurable.

398

The Halle is the Louvre of the people: all the good that is achieved there benefits the sovereign.

399

Death is sleep without dreams, and perhaps without an awakening.

400

A man made for business and authority never sees people, but things and their consequences.

401

Physical faculties are sharpened and enlarged in the midst of peril and need; sailors and Bedouins have the eyes of lynxes, and the forest savages have the noses of beasts.

402

A long and voluminous ministerial correspondence is an arsenal in which there are blades with all sorts of edges.

403

You can make courtiers with ribbons – you cannot make men.

404

Nothing which degrades man is useful for long.

405

The falsest of politics is the one which opposes one faction to the other while priding itself on diminishing both.

406

The man of power is the one who can intercept at will the communication between the senses and thought.

407

A king is accountable every day.

408

Fate is the result of a calculation of which we do not yet know all the data.

409

A superior power pushes me towards a goal of which I know nothing; as long as it has not been attained I am invulnerable, unshakeable; as soon as I am no longer necessary for it, a single step will suffice to topple me.

410
Nothing more difficult than coming to a decision.

411
The inevitable fate of large groups is to perish because of lack of unity.

412
Inspiring confidence before success is the most difficult political task.

413
In the position I am in, I can see nobility only in the rabble I have neglected, and rabble only in the nobility I have created. (*1814*)

414
Only General Bonaparte can save the Emperor Napoleon. (*1818*)

415

He who at any moment stands to lose everything must risk everything at any moment.

416

Great powers die of indigestion.

417

There is neither absolute happiness nor absolute unhappiness in the world: the life of a happy man is a picture with a silver background with black stars; the life of an unhappy man is a black background with silver stars.

418

A king must not descend beneath adversity.

419

It was not I who missed the soldiers, but the soldiers who missed me. (*1814*)

420

Absolute power has no need to lie: it acts and stays silent. A responsible government is always obliged to speak and ends up telling horrible lies: in no time at all it is discredited, it falls to general contempt. At least absolute power falls to general hatred.

421

You can stop while ascending, never while descending.

422

Despite what Machiavelli says, fortresses are not worth more than the support of the people.

423

There are no more people's rights in Europe: it is all about scrapping with one another like dogs.

424

Oppressing the masses while giving the most amount of freedom to individuals is the secret of governments which will succeed me: selfishness is the only motive. I have been defeated for having attempted to bring about the good of the masses by sacrificing the individual to them.

425

Capability and means are now so common among the people at large that the idea of competition should be avoided – and that is also when, above all, the idea of election should be abandoned.

426

Borrowing is the demise of agricultural nations and the survival of manufacturing nations.

427

Thrones cannot be repaired.

428

It is not what is prohibited, but prohibition itself which causes the crime.

429

Governments with checks and balances are only good during peacetime.

430

Political laws can have no lifespan compared to those of mankind; they are tailored to habit, and habits change.

431

You must respect in their downfall those who are respected in their grandeur.

432

The greatest affliction of politics is that it has no fixed precepts.

433

Happiness depends on events, bliss depends on affections.

434

A society without passions is static.

435

Revolution must learn to predict nothing.

436

France will only die because of Paris.

437

I have been buried along with my entire head.
(*On St Helena*)

438

Chance is the only legitimate king in the universe.

439

My guard was my reserve of men. (*On St Helena*)

440

By launching themselves at me, the Kings have fallen with me.

441

Historical truth is often an accepted myth: in every affair there is the material fact and the intention; the fact which should be incontrovertible is often a never-ending process. How then can one speak of the underlying intentions afterwards? I have found my own thoughts about a battle being contested.

442

I sunk at the sail, with the world in steerage. (*On St Helena*)

443

There is no theft, everything is paid for.

444

Ideas mature in success as well as in distress.

445

There can be no republic in France: republicans of good faith are idiots, the others are fools or plotters.

446

It is quite difficult to govern in good conscience.

447

You can give a first impulse to affairs – afterwards
they pull you along.

448

It is always vile and dishonourable to slander the
unfortunate.

449

A strike of fate is like that of the die on the coin:
it marks a man according to his value.

450

Under a government of action, only material
forces count.

451

France loves change too much for a government
to last.

452

The human spirit has achieved three victories:
the jury system, equal taxation and freedom of
conscience.

453

With a sincere ally, France would be master of the world.

454

Constant devotion is the rarest thing in the world.

455

Superstition is the legacy left by one century's clever people to the fools of the future.

456

When the soldiers have received their baptism of fire, they are all equal in front of me. (*On St Helena, speaking of the British soldiers guarding him*)

457

Solon* and Egypt were right: you cannot judge a man until after his death.

458

You can rise above those who insult you by forgiving them.

459

As a rule, you must always reserve the right to laugh the next day at your thoughts of the previous night.

460

Government is a necessary evil.

461

There is more chance of getting a good sovereign by inheritance than by election.

462

Nobody has seen in my war of Spain an intention to possess the Mediterranean.

463

I do not have too much of anything but time. (*On St Helena*)

464

Oligarchies never change opinion: their interests are always the same.

465

How many high-ranking men become children several times a day?

466

Populations can recover from all setbacks when they occupy a large area.

467

Every age confers another role on us.

468

In fifty years, Europe will either be republican or Cossack. (*On St Helena*)

469

My wars have killed all parchments.

470

The cannon killed the feudal system, ink will kill modern society.

471

Chance accounts for all our foolishness.

472

The characteristic of a state is to announce its own demise.

473

The French have no nationality. (*Maybe he meant patriotism?*)

474

No human institution can last if it is based on sentiment.

475

There is as much courage in suffering with tenacity the hardships of life as in staying rooted behind battery fortifications.

476

To be deprived of your childhood room, of the garden in which you roamed in your early years, not to have a paternal home, is to have no homeland.

477

Money or ribbons: the ribbons will wear out, governing will become more expensive.

478

The French will be worth their salt when they substitute principles for turbulence, pride for vanity, love of institutions for love of rank.

479

The follies of others never make us wise.

480

Political equilibrium is a pipe dream.

481

A single man cannot manage to organize an old and revolutionized country.

482

The constitutionalists are dupes: all pacts in France have been broken, and will be broken again: they are merely written on paper.

483

In the long run, too much power ends up corrupting the most honest of men.

484

My history is made up of events which mere words cannot destroy.

485

The colonial system is finished; we should stick to free navigation of the oceans and universal free trade.

486

At Waterloo, everything started to fail only once everything had succeeded.

487

The old system is nearing its end, and the new one has no chance, because a responsible government will always lack unity.

488

Democracy can be furious, but it has guts, it can be roused; for the aristocracy it always remains cold and unforgiving.

489

I have planted principles into the Italians which will never be uprooted; they will always be maturing.

490

France has natural boundaries that I have never wanted to cross; I wanted to make Italy an independent kingdom.

491

Antwerp was a constantly loaded pistol pointed at the heart of England.

492

A ministry can withstand setbacks that would kill a sovereign.

493

Of all aristocracies, that of money is the worst.

494

These days the throne is a magistrature rather than a lordship.

495

Our body is a machine for living.

496

If you are a successful conqueror, you must be ferocious.

497

Declamations come and go; actions remain.

498

The Kings will pay dearly for my demise.

499

Even in its most corrupt moments, baseness has its limits.

500

If the vast majority of society decided to misread the laws, who would have the power to stop it?

501

Misfortune has its own heroism.

502

If I had died in an aura of omnipotence, I would have remained a problem; thanks to my deportation I can be judged naked.

503

After my abdication, France was forced with a foot on its throat to raise fifteen hundred million; England voluntarily raised seven billion.

504

In former times only one type of property was known: land; a new kind then appeared:

industry, which at present is grappling with the first one; then a third one, which derives from the enormous levies collected from the governed masses and which, distributed by the neutral and impartial hands of government, can guarantee the monopoly of the other two, serve as their intermediary and prevent them from coming to blows. However, since we do not to recognize this great revolution in property and keep turning a blind eye to such truths, we commit so much foolishness today and are exposed to so much upheaval. The world has experienced a great shift, and it is trying to settle down again – this, in a word, is the entire key to the universal unrest that is tormenting us.

The vessel has been undocked, ballast has been carried from the front to the back, and from there stem the furious oscillations which may lead to shipwreck at the first sign of a storm, if we persist in wanting to manoeuvre as usual, without having achieved a new balance.

505

As long as I stayed at the head of state affairs,
France was in the same state as Rome when
it was declared that a dictator was needed to
rescue it: one had to overthrow in order not to
be overthrown.

506

Whoever ends up possessing Constantinople
will govern the world.

507

I never wanted to shape events around my
system, on the contrary: I shaped my system
around the unforeseen combination of events.

508

My iron fist was not situated at the end of my
arm, it was directly attached to my head: it was
calculation and not nature which had given it to
me.

509

The first sovereign who, in the middle of the first great struggle, embraces the cause of the people in good faith, will find himself at the head of Europe.

510

One of my first grand ideas was the consolidation, the concentration of the same geographic peoples who were dispersed and fragmented by revolutions and politics. In Europe there are thirty million French, fifteen million Spaniards, fifteen million Italians, thirty million Germans and twenty million Poles; I wanted to make of each one nation. The impulse has been given; each of these revolutions will come about, and it is my idea which can serve as a lever for the future destinies of Europe.

511

I was forced to fight for ten years on the corpses of the Germans; they could never know my true intentions for them, which were ambitious.

512

There are no great sustained actions which are the product of chance or fortune; they always derive from the machinations of genius.

513

By not resuscitating Poland, Lord Castlereagh has handed Constantinople to Russia, exposed all of Europe and sowed the seeds of a thousand embarrassments for England.

514

It took me fifteen years to re-establish the Italian nationality.

515

Russia must fall or expand. If it succeeds in incorporating Poland by reconciling the Poles with its government, it will have made the biggest step towards the conquest of India; if it alienates them, it will always be threatened behind its back.

516

Russia is all the more formidable in that it never disarms.

517

Russia will take over Constantinople and a large part of Turkey. I consider it as certain as if it had already happened (*1817*). Once in Constantinople, it will become a maritime power, and God knows what will come next.

518

If Hannibal had been defeated at the Trebbia, at Trasimeno and at Cannes, nothing like the disasters which followed Zama would have happened.

519

My assassination at Schönbrunn would have been less fatal than my marriage to Marie-Louise.

520

The only conquests that leave no regrets are the ones made in ignorance.

521

Britain settles its commerce with India with blood.

522

Britain is the only power that would benefit from France not having Belgium, and as long as it will not let it possess it, there will be no sincerity in its alliance.

523

It is unjust for a generation to be indebted to the previous one; a loan should be limited to fifty years. Why should the people, who are not responsible for the debts of the deceased king, not have the privilege of the crown? A means to preserve coming generations from the greed of previous generations must be found, without having to resort to bankruptcy.

524

I would never have wanted to take out a loan. In 1814, France only had sixty million to pay in bonds, and I left more than one hundred million of my own money.

525

A new Prometheus, I am attached to a rock where a vulture is gnawing at me. I had stolen the fire of heaven to endow France with it; the fire has come back to its source, and here I am.

Notes

p. 70, *Gall*: Franz Joseph Gall (1758–1828), the German physiologist who originated phrenology.

p. 86, *Solon*: Solon (*c.*630 BC–*c.*560 BC), the Athenian statesman renowned for his wisdom.

Biographical Note

NAPOLEON BONAPARTE was born on 15th August 1769 in Ajaccio, Corsica to Carlo Buonaparte, a lawyer, and Letizia Ramolino. In 1778 Napoleon was admitted to the Collège d'Autun in Paris, after which he was educated at military academies in Brienne and Paris. In 1785 Carlo died, leaving Napoleon as the head of the household. Napoleon trained as an artillery officer, and in 1792 was made a captain. In 1793, he directed the artillery in the siege of Toulon. When the city fell, he was given command of the artillery of the army in Italy. Part of the reason for his advancement was his allegiance to the Jacobins, so when they fell from power his command was taken from him, and he returned to Paris.

In October 1795, the people of Paris rose against the authorities. Napoleon, now Brigadier General, successfully repressed the revolt, for which he was rewarded by being made commander of the army in Italy. He pursued a highly effective campaign against the Austrians, which ended in their defeat.

After a triumphant return to Paris, he took a large army to Egypt. He planned to emulate the achievements of Alexander the Great. However, midway through the campaign, unrest in France prompted his return. The authorities had lost popular approval. Napoleon joined a plot to overthrow them, and was appointed ruler of the country, with the title of Consul. Later, in 1804, he crowned himself as Emperor of France, and in 1805 was crowned King of Italy with the Iron Crown of Lombardy.

As a ruler, he formed incredibly ambitious plans to enlarge the French territory. He also significantly reformed French society, most importantly with the Code Napoléon, a codification of French law which has strongly influenced the law-making of numerous other countries.

In 1805 England were joined by Russia, Austria and Sweden in the Third Coalition against France. Napoleon planned to invade England, but was thwarted by Britain's victory at the Battle of Trafalgar, which gave the Royal Navy control of the seas. However, he defeated Austria and Russia at the Battle of Austerlitz, one of his most famous victories, which effectively ended the Third Coalition. Austria signed the Peace of Pressburg with France, which led to the Confederation of the Rhine, with Napoleon appointed as Protector. After the Peace of Pressburg, England was the only country still at war with France.

The following year, The Fourth Coalition, consisting of Prussia, Russia, Saxony, Sweden and England, was assembled. After defeating Prussia and Russia, Napoleon signed the Treaties of Tilsit with these countries. The treaties made France and Russia into the most powerful countries in Europe, as well as forging an alliance between them.

Napoleon's military successes, in which his skill as a strategist and tactician played a large part, achieved some of his ambitions for extending the French Empire – at its height, it included France up to the Rhine, Belgium, Holland, some parts of Italy, Croatia and Dalmatia.

Napoleon's first marriage to Joséphine de Beauharnais had been childless. As he was now

Emperor, he was able to hand the throne down to his descendants. So he divorced Joséphine in 1809, and in 1810 married Marie Louise, the eighteen-year-old daughter of the Emperor of Austria, who within a year gave him a son.

Napoleon put forward a Continental system – an embargo against England's trade with the rest of Europe. However, most countries objected to the system, and found ways of getting round it. This included Russia. The defection prompted him to turn against Russia, and invade it.

The campaign ended in disaster. The Russians avoided a decisive conflict, and drew him deeper into Russian territory. Their scorched-earth tactics and severe climate conditions put the French at a great disadvantage. After an inconclusive conflict at Borodino, the Russians retreated beyond Moscow. Napoleon expected the city's capture would be the end of the war, and that he could replenish supplies there. But when he arrived, the city had been burned down by the Russians. At this point Napoleon retreated. The French army suffered an enormous number of casualties during the retreat, which has been called one of the greatest disasters in military history.

The Sixth Coalition was formed by Russia, England, Spain, Portugal, Sweden and Austria. They defeated Napoleon at the Battle of Leipzig in 1813. He retreated into France. The Coalition invaded, and captured Paris in 1814. Napoleon's generals refused to continue the conflict, and he was forced to abdicate.

Napoleon was exiled to the island of Elba. However, after ten months, he escaped and returned to France. He rallied his supporters, and for a brief time resumed his command of France. But this period ended with the Battle of Waterloo in 1815, in which he was defeated by England and Prussia.

He was exiled to the island of St Helena, where he died in 1821.

HONORÉ DE BALZAC was born in Tours, France, on 20th May 1799. He produced a vast body of prose works collectively known as *La Comédie humaine* ("The Human Comedy"), intended to capture realistically every aspect of contemporary life. He is generally regarded as one of the founders of realism, and one of the greatest novelists of all time. He died on 18th August 1850 in Paris.

Note on the Text

The translated text in the present edition is based on the 1838 edition of *Maximes et pensées de Napoléon*, published by Barbier in Paris and compiled purportedly by a J.-L. Gaudy, but generally believed to be the work of the writer Honoré de Balzac.

ONEWORLD CLASSICS

ONEWORLD CLASSICS aims to publish mainstream and lesser-known European classics in an innovative and striking way, while employing the highest editorial and production standards. By way of a unique approach the range offers much more, both visually and textually, than readers have come to expect from contemporary classics publishing.

❧

ANTON CHEKHOV: *Sakhalin Island*
Translated by Brian Reeve

ANTON CHEKHOV: *The Woman in the Case*
Translated by Kyril FitzLyon

CHARLES DICKENS: *The Haunted House*

D.H. LAWRENCE: *The First Women in Love*

D.H. LAWRENCE: *Paul Morel*

JAMES HANLEY: *Boy*

JACK KEROUAC: *Beat Generation*

GIUSEPPE GIOACCHINO BELLI: *Sonnets*
Translated by Mike Stocks

GIACOMO LEOPARDI: *Canti*
Translated by J.G. Nichols

HENRY MILLER: *Quiet Days in Clichy*

FRANZ KAFKA: *Letter to My Father*
Translated by Hannah Stokes

GIOVANNI BOCCACCIO: *Decameron*
Translated by J.G. Nichols

GIOVANNI BOCCACCIO: *Life of Dante*

DANTE ALIGHIERI: *Rime*
Translated by A. Mortimer and J.G. Nichols

IVAN BUNIN: *Dark Avenues*
Translated by Hugh Aplin

FYODOR DOSTOEVSKY: *Humiliated and Insulted*
Translated by Ignat Avsey

ÉMILE ZOLA: *Ladies' Delight*
Translated by April Fitzlyon

BOILEAU: *The Art of Poetry* and *Lutrin*
Translated by William Soames and John Ozell

CECCO ANGIOLIERI: *Sonnets*
Translated by C.H. Scott

STENDHAL: *The Life of Rossini*
Translated by Richard N. Coe

GOETHE: *Kindred by Choice*
Translated by H.M. Waidson

POPE: *The Art of Sinking in Poetry*

DROSTE-HÜLSHOFF: *The Jew's Beech*
Translated by Lionel and Doris Thomas

MIKHAIL BULGAKOV: *The Master and Margarita*
Translated by Hugh Aplin

MÖRIKE: *Mozart's Journey to Prague*
Translated by L. von Loewenstein-Wertheim

CHAMISSO: *Peter Schlemihl*
Translated by L. von Loewenstein-Wertheim

MÉRIMÉE: *A Slight Misunderstanding*
Translated by Douglas Parmée

ROUSSEL: *Locus Solus*
Translated by Rupert Copeland Cuningham

ERASMUS: *Praise of Folly*
Translated by Roger Clarke

CALDER PUBLICATIONS

Since 1949, john calder has published eighteen Nobel Prize winners and around fifteen hundred books. He has put into print many of the major French and European writers, almost single-handedly introducing modern literature into the English language. His commitment to literary excellence has influenced two generations of authors, readers, booksellers and publishers. We are delighted to keep John Calder's legacy alive and hope to honour his achievements by continuing his tradition of excellence into a new century.

～

ANTONIN ARTAUD: *The Theatre and Its Double*

CÉLINE: *Journey to the End of the Night*

CÉLINE: *Death on Credit*

MARGUERITE DURAS: *The Sailor from Gibraltar*

MARGUERITE DURAS: *Moderato Cantabile*

ERICH FRIED: *100 Poems without a Country*

ERICH FRIED: *Love Poems*

EUGÈNE IONESCO: *Plays*

LUIGI PIRANDELLO: *Collected Plays*

RAYMOND QUENEAU: *Exercises in Style*

ALAIN ROBBE-GRILLET: *In the Labyrinth*

ALEXANDER TROCCHI: *Cain's Book*

To order any of our titles and for up-to-date information about our current and forthcoming publications, please visit our website on:

www.oneworldclassics.com